The Hidden Chambers Underneath Giza

By *Mike Bhangu*

BBP Copyright 2025

Copyright © 2025 by Mike Bhangu.

This book is licensed and is being offered for your personal enjoyment only. It is prohibited for this book to be re-sold, shared and/or to be given away to other people. If you would like to provide and/or share this book with someone else, please purchase an additional copy. If you did not personally purchase this book for your own personal enjoyment and are reading it, please respect the hard work of this author and purchase a copy for yourself.

All rights reserved. No part of this book may be used or reproduced or transmitted in any manner whatsoever without written permission from the author, except for the inclusion of brief quotations in reviews, articles, and recommendations. Thank you for honoring this.

Published by BB Productions
British Columbia, Canada
thinkingmanmike@gmail.com

The Hidden Chambers
Underneath Giza

Table of Contents

Chapter 1: The Modern Mystery – Or, How to Lose Your Mind in 4,500 Years

Chapter 2: The Prophets of Atlantis – Or, How to Nap Your Way to Fame

Chapter 3: Thoth/Hermes Trismegistus – The OG Guru Who Couldn't Stop Multitasking

Chapter 4: The Egyptian Underworld – Or, How to Die and Still Have a To-Do List

Chapter 5: Cross-Cultural Underground Realms – Or, Why Every Culture Has a Basement Full of Drama

Chapter 6: The Tech of Discovery – Or, How to Spy on Pyramids Without Leaving Your Couch

Chapter 7: Egyptology's Perspective – Or, How to Kill a Vibe in 10 Syllables or Less

Chapter 8: Bridging Myth and Reality – Or, How to Gaslight Yourself into Believing in Atlantis

Chapter 9: The Ethics of Exploration – Or, How to Not Get Cursed in 5 Easy Steps

Chapter 10: A Nexus of Science and Spirituality – Or, How to Hug It Out with a Pyramid

Chapter 1: The Modern Mystery

- Recent discoveries: The "Big Void," ScanPyramids anomalies, and ground-penetrating radar findings.

- Media frenzy and public imagination: Why hidden chambers captivate us.

- Introduction to the *Emerald Tablets of Thoth the Atlantean* and Maurice Doreal's claims about Giza's subterranean secrets.

Chapter 2: The Prophets of Atlantis

- Edgar Cayce's "Hall of Records" prophecy and its ties to Atlantis.

- Maurice Doreal's *Emerald Tablets*: A 20th-century mythos of Thoth, Atlantis, and cosmic archives.

- The cultural impact of New Age theories on archaeology.

Chapter 3: The Wisdom of Thoth

- Thoth/Hermes Trismegistus in Egyptian and Hermetic traditions.

- The ancient *Emerald Tablet* and its alchemical maxims ("As above, so below").

- The *Corpus Hermeticum* and the idea of hidden temple wisdom.

Chapter 4: The Egyptian Underworld and the Duat

- The *Book of the Dead* and the journey through the Duat.

- Symbolism of subterranean realms: Are they metaphors or physical places?

- Medieval Arab accounts (e.g., Al-Maqrizi) of tunnels and treasures beneath Giza.

Chapter 5: Cross-Cultural Underground Realms

- Hindu *Patala* and the Nagas: Advanced beings beneath the Earth.

- Plato's Atlantis and its imagined connection to Giza.
- Gnostic "treasure houses" and Coptic Christian legends of hidden knowledge.

Chapter 6: The Technology of Discovery
- Modern tools: Muon radiography, LiDAR, and ground-penetrating radar.
- Case studies: The "Big Void," Osiris Shaft, and other anomalies.
- Challenges of interpreting data: Structural gaps vs. intentional chambers.

Chapter 7: Egyptology's Perspective
- Mainstream theories: Pyramids as tombs and spiritual monuments.
- Scholarly critiques of Atlantis and "Hall of Records" claims.
- The role of Occam's Razor in archaeological interpretation.

Chapter 8: Bridging Myth and Reality
- Parallels between ancient texts and modern discoveries: Coincidence or collective memory?
- The psychological appeal of hidden knowledge and lost civilizations.
- Could future excavations validate esoteric narratives?

Chapter 9: The Ethics of Exploration
- Balancing preservation with curiosity: Should we drill into the "Big Void"?
- UNESCO and Egypt's stance on invasive investigations.
- Lessons from past controversies (e.g., the Osiris Shaft excavations).

Chapter 10: A Nexus of Science and Spirituality

- The pyramids as symbols of humanity's quest for meaning.
- Reconciling empiricism with myth: A new framework for ancient mysteries.
- Speculative futures: What if the "Hall of Records" is real?

Chapter 1: The Modern Mystery – Or, How to Lose Your Mind in 4,500 Years

The "Big Void" – Not Just a Tuesday Night Feeling
Let's kick things off with the star of the show: the Big Void. No, it's not the existential dread you feel scrolling through Instagram at 2 a.m. It's a massive, unexplained *nothingness* inside the Great Pyramid of Giza, discovered in 2017 by scientists using muon radiography. (Yes, "muon radiography" sounds like a spell from *Harry Potter*, but it's real. Scientists shoot cosmic particles through stone like tiny X-ray ghosts. Take that, Hogwarts!)

This void is roughly the size of a Boeing 747 and has archaeologists scratching their heads harder than a toddler with lice. Is it a secret chamber? A structural accident? Khufu's ancient walk-in closet? Nobody knows! But hey, it's the most exciting non-answer since your partner said, "We need to talk" and then asked you to fold laundry.

The ScanPyramids Project: Science, Sand, and Serious Side-Eye
Enter the ScanPyramids Project, a team of international scientists armed with gadgets fancier than a Bond villain's espresso machine. Their mission: to scan Egypt's pyramids without, you know, *actually touching them*. Because apparently, after 4,500 years, the pyramids are like that one friend who says, "I'm not mad, just disappointed" if you move their couch.

Using thermal cameras, LiDAR, and ground-penetrating radar, they've found:

- Anomalies (fancy science talk for "stuff that's not rock").
- Tunnels that might lead to chambers or might lead to a very disappointed mummy yelling, "Can't a guy nap in peace?!"
- More questions than a toddler at a zoo.

But here's the kicker: Egypt's Ministry of Antiquities is like, "Cool story, bro. Now *hands off*." Because poking holes in pyramids is frowned upon, even if you're 99% sure there's a room full of alien Wi-Fi routers down there.

Maurice Doreal's Wild Ride: Thoth, Atlantis, and Chill
Now, let's talk about Maurice Doreal, the 1930s mystic who wrote *The Emerald Tablets of Thoth the Atlantean*. Picture a guy who's equal parts Indiana Jones and your weird uncle who won't stop talking about lizard people. According to Doreal, Thoth (an immortal Atlantean priest-king with better hair than Jason Momoa) hid a Hall of Records under Giza. This hall supposedly holds:

- Atlantean archives (think *Library of Alexandria* meets *Black Panther*'s Wakanda).
- Advanced technology (probably powered by crystals and vibes).
- Cosmic wisdom (or as I call it, "the ultimate self-help book").

Scholars roll their eyes so hard they risk retinal detachment, but *come on*. If Netflix optioned this, it'd be a six-season hit with a rushed finale.

Edgar Cayce: The Prophet Who Napped Too Hard

No pyramid mystery is complete without Edgar Cayce, the "Sleeping Prophet" who took naps so intense he hallucinated Atlantis. Cayce claimed there's a Hall of Records under the Sphinx's paw, guarded by a trapdoor that's "definitely not cursed, probably." (Spoiler: It's cursed.)

Modern archaeologists haven't found it yet, but Cayce fans are still holding out hope, muttering, "Just wait till Season 3 of *Ancient Aliens*."

Why We Care: Humans Love a Good Plot Twist

Why are we obsessed with hidden chambers? Simple: we're nosy. We're the same species that invented reality TV and Twitter. The pyramids are the ultimate cold case—*CSI: Nile Delta*. We've got:
- Ancient riddles ("Why build a tomb with more tunnels than a gopher convention?").
- High-tech tools that make us feel like geniuses until we realize we still can't open a PDF.
- The nagging fear that maybe, just maybe, the ancients were trolling us.

Chapter 2: The Prophets of Atlantis – Or, How to Nap Your Way to Fame

Edgar Cayce: The Sleeping Prophet Who Dreamed of Atlantis (and Probably Unpaid Bills)

Edgar Cayce (1877–1945) was a Kentucky-born mystic who could've been the love child of Sherlock Holmes and a sloth. Known as the "Sleeping Prophet", he'd lie down, take a *nap*, and wake up spouting prophecies, medical advice, and casual revelations about Atlantis. Think of him as the original *influencer*—except instead of TikTok dances, he gave existential dread.

- Early Life: Grew up on a farm, claimed to see angels (or maybe just really convincing fireflies).
- Career: Failed photographer, failed insurance salesman, *wildly successful* psychic.
- Signature Move: Trance-induced "readings" where he diagnosed illnesses and prescribed things like "atomic iodine" and "peanut oil massages" (the OG essential oils MLM).
- Legacy: 14,000+ documented readings, a cult following, and a permanent spot on the "Wait, *What?*" shelf of history.

Cayce's Greatest Hit: The Hall of Records™

While snoozing in 1933, Cayce declared that a Hall of Records—a library of Atlantis's greatest hits—lay buried under the Sphinx's left paw. According to him, this vault contained:

- Crystal tablets sharper than your aunt's Twitter takes.
- Advanced tech (probably powered by vibes and pyramid energy).
- Proof that Atlantis was *real* and definitely not just Plato's fanfiction.

Scholars scoffed, but Cayce fans were like, "Trust the process!" Fast-forward to today: we've scanned the Sphinx's paws, found *nothing*, and now everyone's arguing if the Hall is "metaphorical" or if Cayce just forgot to say "PSYCH!"

Maurice Doreal: The Man Who Wrote Fanfiction Before It Was Cool

Meet Maurice Doreal (real name: Claude Doggins, because *obviously*). This 1930s mystic looked like a cross between a jazz musician and a wizard who shops at Hot Topic. He wrote *The Emerald Tablets of Thoth the Atlantean*, a text so extra it makes *The Da Vinci Code* look like a grocery list.

Key Claims (With a Side of Eye-Roll):

- Thoth was an immortal Atlantean priest-king who fled to Egypt after Atlantis pulled a *Titanic*.
- He buried a Hall of Records under Giza, filled with "cosmic wisdom" (read: ancient Wikipedia).

- The chambers include "halls of light" and "chambers of darkness," which sound like a rave venue run by Daft Punk.

Scholars: "This is fiction."
Doreal Fans: "But what if... *aliens*?"

The Hall of Records: Atlantis's Dropbox (Still Buffering)
Both Cayce and Doreal's Hall of Records is the ultimate MacGuffin—a plot device that keeps us hooked despite zero evidence. Imagine if *National Treasure*'s Nicolas Cage teamed up with a guy who thinks "the mitochondria is the powerhouse of the cell" is a prophecy.

Why These Guys Matter: The Power of a Good Story
Let's be real: Cayce and Doreal were the Ancient Aliens of their time. They tapped into humanity's love affair with:
1. Secret Knowledge (because Googling "how to adult" is too mainstream).
2. Collapsing Civilizations (Atlantis: the original "we have food at home").
3. The Thrill of Being Wrong (see: flat-Earthers, anti-vaxxers, and people who think *Friends* is still funny).

Their tales endure because *mystery sells*. Who needs facts when you have drama, crystals, and the chance to yell "I told you so!" at smug archaeologists?

The Hidden Chambers Underneath Giza

Sidebar: Edgar Cayce's Greatest Hits (Besides Napping)

1. Medical Advice: Prescribed "ash of burnt wine barrels" for ulcers. Side effects may include *death* or a killer hangover.
2. Predictions: Foresaw stock market crashes, WWII, and California sinking into the ocean (2 out of 3 ain't bad).
3. Atlantis Lore: Claimed Atlanteans used "fire crystals" for energy. So, basically, they had *lightsabers*.

Mike Bhangu

Chapter 3: Thoth/Hermes Trismegistus – The OG Guru Who Couldn't Stop Multitasking

Thoth: The Egyptian God Who Invented Homework (Probably)
Meet Thoth—the ancient Egyptian deity who moonlighted as the universe's ultimate overachiever. Imagine if Elon Musk, Shakespeare, and Gandalf had a baby who *also* invented the calendar. That's Thoth.

- Day Job: Moon god, scribe of the underworld, and patron of *literally everyone who's ever cried over a deadline*.
- Hobbies: Inventing hieroglyphs (the original emojis), judging souls (Egyptian *Shark Tank*), and babysitting the sun god Ra.
- Signature Move: Writing the *Book of the Dead* like it's a Yelp review for the afterlife: ★★★★☆ "Would recommend, but the boat ride across the Nile is overpriced."
- Fun Fact: Depicted as an ibis (a bird that looks like it's perpetually judging your life choices) or a baboon (because why not?).

Thoth's resume is so stacked, even LinkedIn would say, "Chill, dude."

Hermes Trismegistus: When Thoth Got a Greek Makeover
Fast-forward to ancient Greece, where someone went, "Thoth's cool, but what if we... *rebrand him*?" Enter Hermes Trismegistus—a mashup of

Thoth and Hermes (the Greek god of messengers, thieves, and side hustles). Think of him as the *Avengers: Endgame* of mythology, but with more togas and fewer explosions.

- Name Meaning: "Thrice-Great Hermes" (because "Twice-Great" was taken).
- Claim to Fame: Writing the *Hermetica*, a series of texts that blend philosophy, astrology, and advice on how to turn lead into gold (spoiler: you can't).
- Legacy: Inspired alchemists, Renaissance nerds, and that guy at the coffee shop who won't shut up about "vibrations."

The Emerald Tablet: Ancient TikTok Wisdom

The *Emerald Tablet* is Hermes Trismegistus's greatest hit—a cryptic one-pager that's basically the *"Live, Laugh, Love"* of alchemy. Its most famous line: "As above, so below." Translation: "The universe is a cosmic mirror, so if your life's a mess, blame the stars."

Key Takeaways (If You're High Enough):
1. Everything's connected. Your cat, the moon, that burrito you ate—*all one vibe*.
2. To understand the universe, just vibe harder.
3. If you figure it out, you'll turn lead into gold. If not, you'll turn ramen into regret.

Medieval alchemists treated this like the *Da Vinci Code*, but instead of Tom Hanks, you get a bunch of dudes in robes yelling, "I'M SO CLOSE!"

Hermeticism: The Original Self-Help Cult

Hermes Trismegistus's fan club, Hermeticism, was the ancient world's answer to Goop. Followers believed:
- The universe is a mind game created by God's ADHD.
- Humans can become gods through *~knowledge~* and *~magic~* (or at least get better at trivia night).
- The secret to immortality is written down *somewhere*, probably under a pyramid.

Renaissance bigwigs like Leonardo da Vinci and Isaac Newton were low-key obsessed. Newton spent years trying to decode the *Emerald Tablet* instead of, say, inventing something useful, like Wi-Fi.

Thoth's Greatest Hits (Besides Side-Eyeing Ra)

1. Invented Writing: So humanity could stop yelling "BRB" across the desert.
2. Mediated Drama: Settled fights between gods like a celestial HR rep. (Set: "You stole my throne!" Horus: "You started it!" Thoth: "Cool story. Write it down.")
3. Designed the Calendar: Because even gods need due dates for *"smite mortals"* on their to-do lists.

Why Thoth/Hermes Still Matters: The Ultimate Flex

Thoth/Hermes is the patron saint of nerds who won't shut up. His legacy lives on in:

- Tarot Cards: The "Magician" card? That's him. *"Look at my cool hat!"*
- Alchemy Memes: Turning mercury into gold? More like turning crypto into debt.
- New Age TikTok: Where teens use his quotes as captions for sunset selfies.

Sidebar: Thoth vs. Hermes Trismegistus – Fight!

- Thoth: "I invented writing, judged souls, and kept the moon on schedule. Bow down."
- Hermes Trismegistus: "I'm *literally* you but with better PR. Also, here's a recipe for philosopher's stone soufflé."

Chapter 4: The Egyptian Underworld – Or, How to Die and Still Have a To-Do List

The *Book of the Dead*: Ancient Egypt's Ultimate Checklist
Imagine dying and your afterlife depends on *paperwork*. That's right—welcome to ancient Egypt, where death was less "rest in peace" and more "rest in bureaucracy." The *Book of the Dead* (or, as I call it, *"Dummies Guide to Not Getting Eaten by a Hippo God"*) was your VIP pass through the Duat, the Egyptian underworld. Think of it as a mix between *SAT prep*, *The Amazing Race*, and a Yelp review for the afterlife:

- Step 1: Die. (Easy enough!)
- Step 2: Memorize 200+ spells to dodge demons, scales, and gods with anger issues.
- Step 3: Convince Osiris, the green-skinned CEO of the afterlife, that you *didn't* steal your neighbor's goat. (Spoiler: You totally stole the goat.)

If you passed, congrats! You got eternal paradise. If not, your soul got devoured by Ammit, a demon that's part lion, part hippo, part crocodile, and 100% why Egyptians needed therapy.

The Duat: Hell's Theme Park (With a Gift Shop)
The Duat wasn't some gloomy cave—it was a spiritual obstacle course with more twists than a Netflix thriller. Highlights included:

- Lake of Fire: Not a metaphor. Just, you know, *fire*.
- 12 Gates Guarded by Snakes: Because regular doormen weren't terrifying enough.
- The Weighing of the Heart: Where your heart got tossed on a scale against a feather. If your heart was heavier? Too bad—Ammit's snack time. (Pro tip: Lay off the bread and beer in life.)

Egyptians took this so seriously, they buried *cheat sheets* (aka the *Book of the Dead*) with their mummies. Imagine dying and your ghost is like, "Wait, did I pack the spell for *'Avoiding Snake Demons 101'*?!"

Medieval Arab Historians: The Original Conspiracy Theorists
Fast-forward to the Middle Ages, when Arab writers like Al-Maqrizi showed up like, "Hold my falafel—I've got theories." These guys claimed the pyramids weren't just tombs but treasure-filled labyrinths with:
- Tunnels to Nowhere: Perfect for getting lost and questioning your life choices.
- Cursed Chambers: Guarded by "jinn" (genies), because why not add *wish-granting* to the mix?
- Secret Maps: Allegedly drawn by ancient priests who were *really* into *National Treasure* vibes.

Modern archaeologists roll their eyes, but let's be real: If Al-Maqrizi had Twitter, he'd be trending with hashtags like #PyramidGate and #WhereIsTheGold.

Symbolism or Stupidity? The Great Debate

Scholars today argue: Was the Duat a *real place* under Giza or just a metaphor for existential dread? Let's break it down:
- Metaphor Camp: "The Duat represents the soul's journey through—" [*falls asleep*]
- Literal Camp: "There's a 7-Eleven down there selling *Soul Slurpees* and I *will* find it."

Meanwhile, tourists at Giza keep asking, "Is the gift shop in the Duat? Asking for a friend."

Sidebar: How to Survive the Duat (Spoiler: You Won't)
1. Flattery Works: Tell Osiris his beard looks *fabulous*.
2. Bribe the Gods: Offer imaginary bread. (They're into that.)
3. Deny Everything: "Steal a goat? Who, me? Never met a goat."

The Hidden Chambers Underneath Giza

Chapter 5: Cross-Cultural Underground Realms – Or, Why Every Culture Has a Basement Full of Drama

Hinduism's Patala: The OG Subway System (But with More Snakes)
Let's start with Patala, Hinduism's answer to *Stranger Things'* Upside Down, but with better interior design. This subterranean paradise (yes, *paradise*) is home to the Nagas—shape-shifting snake-people who'd rather sip cosmic margaritas than haunt your nightmares.

- VIP Residents: The Nagas, who are basically tech bros with scales. They hoard treasure, control weather, and probably invented yoga pants.
- Architecture: Think *Burning Man* meets *Aquaman's* basement. Gold palaces, gem-encrusted tunnels, and rivers of… something sparkly. (Don't ask.)
- Connection to Giza: Conspiracy theorists swear Patala's tunnels stretch to Egypt, because *of course* ancient snakes had better infrastructure than your city's subway.

Hindus take this seriously. The rest of us are like, "So… snake Airbnb?"

Plato's Atlantis: The World's First Timeshare Scam
Next up: Atlantis, the ancient utopia that sank faster than my will to live at a family reunion. Plato described it as a high-tech island with bull-

themed parties and a *slight* god complex. But when Poseidon got salty (literally), it went *glub-glub* into the ocean.

Modern Theories Include:
- Survivors fled to Giza and built pyramids as a *"We Were Here First"* flex.
- The "Hall of Records" is just Atlantis's Yelp reviews: ★☆☆☆☆ *"Sunk without warning. Would not recommend."*
- Plato's Academy was actually a frat house for philosophers. *"Bro, what if… ETHICS?!"*

Archaeologists: "Atlantis is fiction."

Atlantis Truthers: "That's what *they* want you to think!" (Spoiler: "They" is Big Archaeology.)

Gnostic and Coptic Texts: God's Storage Unit
The Gnostics and Coptic Christians weren't about that *"heaven is up"* life. Nope—they believed divine secrets were buried in underground treasure houses, like God's version of a storage locker you forget to pay rent on.

- Gnostic Gospel of Thomas: "The Kingdom of God is inside you… and also under that rock."

- Coptic Legends: Describe tunnels filled with "light" and "knowledge," which sounds suspiciously like a rave with a philosophy degree.
- Link to Giza: If these texts are right, the Great Pyramid is just a giant "Beware of Dog" sign for spiritual loot.

The Universal Theme: Everyone Loves a Good Basement

Why does every culture have a subterranean obsession? Let's break it down:

- Fear of the Unknown: "What's under there?!"
- Daddy Issues: "My ancestors are judging me from... *checks notes*... a cave?"
- Real Estate Envy: Ancient people were like, "We've got pyramids. What do *you* have? A yurt? Cute."

Theories about Giza's hidden chambers fit right in. Maybe the Nagas, Atlanteans, and Gnostic treasure gnomes are all chilling together under the pyramids, playing *Dungeons & Dragons* and laughing at our muon scans.

Sidebar: Patala's Yelp Reviews

- ★★★★☆ *"Loved the gem waterfalls! Nagas were a bit judgy though."*
- ★☆☆☆☆ *"No Wi-Fi. Snake people kept offering me 'enlightenment.' 0/10."*

Chapter 6: The Tech of Discovery – Or, How to Spy on Pyramids Without Leaving Your Couch

Muon Radiography: Ghostbusters, But for Rocks
Let's kick things off with muon radiography, the scientific equivalent of asking cosmic particles to play *Where's Waldo?* with a pyramid. Muons are like the universe's stray cats—they rain down from space, penetrate solid stone, and occasionally photobomb ancient monuments. Scientists use them to scan pyramids, because apparently, X-rays weren't cool enough.

- How It Works: Shoot muons at the pyramid. If they pass through a void, scientists go, "Ooh, anomaly!" If not, they shrug and blame cosmic weather.
- Biggest Flex: In 2017, muons found the Big Void in the Great Pyramid—a space so large it could fit a Boeing 747, or at least a *really* ambitious Airbnb listing.
- Reality Check: Egyptologists are like, "It's probably just a gap for structural balance." Meanwhile, conspiracy theorists: "It's Atlantis's break room. They have a Keurig in there."

LiDAR: The Overachieving Sibling Who Maps Your Life
Next up: LiDAR, the tech that's basically Google Maps on steroids. Archaeologists strap lasers to planes and drones, then scan entire landscapes like they're trying to 3D-print the planet.

- What It Does: Reveals hidden temples, ancient roads, and that one guy who buried his treasure in 1323 and forgot where.
- Giza's Hot Takes: LiDAR's mapped the plateau so thoroughly, it probably knows the Sphinx's WiFi password. Still no Atlantis, though.
- Side Hustle: Used by your nosy neighbor to count how many times you order Uber Eats.

Ground-Penetrating Radar (GPR): The Ultimate Nosy Neighbor

GPR is the Karen of archaeology—always poking its nose where it doesn't belong. It sends radar waves underground and yells, "I HEARD YOU HAVE SECRETS!"

Finds Include:
- Tunnels (possibly ancient, possibly dug by a very ambitious mole).
- Chambers (or as engineers call them, "structural oopsies").
- Disappointment (99% of the time, it's just rocks. *So many rocks*).

The Osiris Shaft: History's Worst Escape Room

Rediscovered in the '90s, the Osiris Shaft is a 100-foot-deep hole under the Sphinx's causeway that's basically Egypt's way of saying, "Hold my beer."

- Contents: Three chambers, a sarcophagus, and enough mystery to fuel a *Tomb Raider* sequel.
- Theories: Tomb of Osiris? Ancient plumbing? Timeout corner for misbehaving pharaohs?
- Tourist Review: ★★☆☆☆ *"Ladders not included. Bring a flashlight and a therapist."*

Old vs. New Archaeology: From Dynamite to Data

19th-Century Archaeologists: "Let's blow stuff up!" **cough* Giovanni Belzoni *cough\

21st-Century Archaeologists: "Let's gently scan stuff while sipping lattes and tweeting #Science."

- Progress: We've gone from "smash first, ask questions never" to "please don't breathe on the artifacts."
- Irony: Despite all our tech, we still don't know if the Big Void is a royal tomb or Khufu's storage unit for extra sandals.

The Drama: Indiana Jones vs. The Lab Coat Brigade

Public Expectation: *"Find the Hall of Records! There's aliens! Gold! Crystal skulls!"*

Scientists: *"It's... probably just a gap. Here's a 40-page PDF on load-bearing architecture."*

- Conspiracy Theorists: *"Why won't they let us drill into the void?!"*
- Egypt's Ministry of Antiquities: *"Because last time someone 'just looked,' they stole the Sphinx's nose."*

Chapter 7: Egyptology's Perspective – Or, How to Kill a Vibe in 10 Syllables or Less

Mainstream Egyptologists: The Fun Police of Archaeology
Meet the Egyptologists—the people who look at a pyramid and say, "Yep, that's a tomb," like they're identifying a stapler. These scholars have spent decades studying hieroglyphs, pharaohs, and the correct way to pronounce "Tutankhamun" without sounding like a toddler with a lollipop. Their take on Giza's mysteries? *"It's a tomb. Stop overthinking it."*

Key Arguments (With a Side of Sass):
1. Pyramids = Giant Tombs: "They're just really fancy coffins. Imagine if your grandma's grave had a zip line."
2. The Sphinx? "A big lion with a pharaoh's face. Not a portal to Atlantis. *Calm down.*"
3. Hidden Chambers? "Probably structural gaps. Unless Khufu was hoarding ancient Legos, it's *not that deep*."

Conspiracy theorists: *"But what if—"*

Egyptologists: *"No."*

The Occam's Razor Award: Simplest Answer Wins
Egyptology's mantra is Occam's Razor: the idea that the simplest explanation is usually right. For example:

The Hidden Chambers Underneath Giza

- Question: Why build a pyramid?
- Occam's Answer: "To flex on future generations."
- Conspiracy Answer: "To power a crystal death ray for alien overlords."

Spoiler: Egyptologists are *really* into the first one.

Debunking the "Hall of Records" Like a Boss

Let's dissect the Hall of Records theory with the enthusiasm of a teacher grading a 3 a.m. essay:

- Edgar Cayce's Prophecy: "It's under the Sphinx!"
- Zahi Hawass (Egypt's Indiana Jones): **eyeroll* "We've dug there. It's sand. So much sand."
- Maurice Doreal's Fanfiction: "Thoth left cosmic WiFi routers underground!"
- Scholars: "Thoth was a god, not an AT&T technician."

The verdict? The only "Hall of Records" at Giza is the gift shop selling postcards of the Sphinx.

The Alien Theory: A Love Story

Conspiracy Theorists: "Aliens built the pyramids! Humans couldn't lift those stones!"

Egyptologists: "Actually, we've found worker cemeteries, tools, and ancient timecards that say *'8 hours of lifting rocks, 1 hour of complaining about Ra.'*"

Bonus Burn:
- "If aliens built the pyramids, why'd they leave? Did the Wi-Fi suck?"
- "And why no alien hieroglyphs? Just one little *'Greetings from Zeta Reticuli'* would've been nice."

The Sphinx's Nose: History's Coldest Case
Everyone blames Napoleon for shooting off the Sphinx's nose. But Egyptologists are like, "Nope. It was gone by the 15th century. Napoleon was too busy conquering Europe and *not* drawing cartoon pharaohs."

Real Culprits: Probably 1) a 14th-century cleric who hated "idols," or 2) a really ambitious pigeon.

The "Big Void" Drama: Much Ado About Nothing
When scientists found the Big Void in the Great Pyramid, Egyptologists shrugged. "It's a relieving chamber," they said. "Meant to reduce pressure. Like Spanx for pyramids."

Public Reaction: *"But what's INSIDE it?"*
Egyptologists: *"Air. Regret. Maybe a stale baguette from 2500 BCE."*

Why Egyptologists Hate Fun
It's not personal—they're just tired of:
> 1. Aliens Stealing Their Thunder: "We studied for 10 years to learn this. *Respect the grind.*"

2. Clickbait Documentaries: *"Ancient Astronaut Theorists Say YES"* to *everything*. Even my cat says "yes" to treats.
3. People Ignoring the Real Wonders: "The pyramids are cool enough without fake Atlantis lore. Like, did you SEE the mortar they used? *Iconic.*"

Chapter 8: Bridging Myth and Reality – Or, How to Gaslight Yourself into Believing in Atlantis

The Conspiracy Theory Playbook: Ancient Texts as Fanfiction
Let's face it: myths are just ancient fanfiction. The *Emerald Tablets of Thoth*? That's Atlantis erotica. The *Book of the Dead*? A self-insert fic where you're the hero and Ammit's the edgy villain who "just needs a hug." But here's the twist: every time archaeologists find a new void under Giza, conspiracy theorists scream, *"See? The fanfic was REAL!"*

Collective Memory: When Grandpa's Tall Tales Go Global
Scientists have a term for myths that *kinda-sorta* match reality: "collective memory." It's like when your uncle claims he invented the dab in 1987, and you're like, *"Sure, Jan."* But applied to entire civilizations.

Examples:
- Atlantis Sinking: Maybe it's a metaphor for that time the Mediterranean flooded a Costco.
- Hall of Records: Could be a distorted memory of ancient tax archives. (*"King Tut owed 30,000 shekels in back taxes. TRUE STORY."*)
- Underground Realms: Or maybe everyone just hated sunlight and dreamed of basements.

The Hidden Chambers Underneath Giza

Psychology 101: Why We're All Suckers for Secret Knowledge

Humans are hardwired to love mysteries more than cats love knocking things off tables. Here's why:

1. FOMO: *"What if there's a secret chamber and I MISSED IT?"*
2. Daddy Issues: *"Ancient aliens are my real parents!"*
3. Boredom: *"My job's dull, but decoding hieroglyphs about snake gods? NOW we're talking."*

This is why TikTok's algorithm shoves *"Giza's Hidden Truths!!!"* videos at you instead of, say, *"How to File Taxes."*

The "What If?" Game: A Hypothetical Guide to Delusion

What if the Hall of Records is real? Let's spiral:

- Discovery Day: Archaeologists crack open a chamber. Inside: crystal USB drives, a manual titled *"How to Not Screw Up Civilization,"* and a sticky note: *"From Atlantis. LOL, our bad."*
- Immediate Aftermath: Reddit crashes. Zahi Hawass becomes a meme. The History Channel rebrands to *"The Prophecy Channel."*
- Long-Term Effects: We finally learn how to use 100% of our brains (spoiler: it's just *coffee*).

Scholarly Side-Eye: When Myths Meet Peer Review

Academics react to conspiracy theories like your mom reacting to your life choices: *"I'm not mad, just disappointed."*

Scholarly Take:

- *"The 'as above, so below' mantra is about cosmic harmony, not literal underground raves."*
- *"Plato made up Atlantis to troll his students. It worked."*
- *"No, the Sphinx isn't 10,000 years old. Stop emailing me."*

Meanwhile, Graham Hancock is somewhere writing a book called *"Scholars Hate This One Weird Chamber!"*

The Ultimate Plot Twist: What If *We're* the Ancient Ones?

Think about it: in 3,000 years, archaeologists will dig up a Costco and claim it was a *"ritual site for worshipping bulk toilet paper."* Future conspiracy theorists will insist we had anti-gravity carts and that *"Kirkland Signature"* was a god.

Moral of the story: Every generation's facts are the next generation's fanfiction.

Chapter 9: The Ethics of Exploration – Or, How to Not Get Cursed in 5 Easy Steps

Step 1: "Drill, Baby, Drill!" vs. "Hands Off, You Maniacs!"
Imagine you're at a party, and someone yells, *"Let's smash the piñata!"* But the piñata is a 4,500-year-old pyramid, and the candy inside might be cursed. That's the ethics of archaeology in a nutshell.

- Team Drill: *"We need ANSWERS! Let's poke a hole in the Big Void! What's the worst that could happen? A mummy's ghost?"*
- Team Hands Off: *"The worst? Crumbling the last Wonder of the Ancient World into a pile of regret. Also, curses. Definitely curses."*

Scientists are stuck between FOMO and FOCO (Fear of Collapsing Obelisks).

Lessons from the Osiris Shaft: Archaeology's "Hold My Beer" Moment
In the '90s, archaeologists rediscovered the Osiris Shaft, a creepy hole under Giza. They went full *Indiana Jones*, dodging water, scorpions, and probably the ghost of a disgruntled intern.

What We Learned:
- Lesson 1: Ancient Egyptians loved building death traps. *"Stairs? Overrated. Let's use ropes!"*

- Lesson 2: If you find a 100-foot shaft, maybe... don't climb into it?
- Lesson 3: Always pack a snack. And a lawyer.

The Media Circus: When Clickbait Meets Carbon Dating

Every time someone whispers *"hidden chamber,"* the internet loses its mind:

- Headlines: *"Scientists Find Void in Pyramid! Aliens Confirm Divorce!"*
- Public Demand: *"DIG IT UP! We need content for Season 6 of *Ancient Aliens*!"*
- Reality: Scientists sigh and write another paper titled *"No, We're Not Hiding Anything, Stop Asking."*

Curses: Ancient Egypt's Yelp Reviews

Speaking of curses—yes, people still believe in them. The "Curse of the Pharaohs" is basically Yelp for tombs:

- ★☆☆☆☆ *"Opened Tut's tomb. Got a papercut. 1/10, would not tomb raid again."*
- ★★★★★ *"Stole a scarab. Now my cat speaks hieroglyphs. Life-changing!"*

Ethicists argue: *"Curses aren't real, but karma? Oh, she's watching."*

Chapter 10: A Nexus of Science and Spirituality – Or, How to Hug It Out with a Pyramid

The Pyramids: Humanity's Original Group Chat

Let's face it: the pyramids are the ultimate "read receipt" from ancient Egypt. They've been sitting there for 4,500 years, silently judging us like a grandparent who *still* doesn't understand TikTok. But whether you're a lab-coat-wearing scientist or a crystal-toting mystic, we all agree on one thing: *they're really freaking cool*.

Science Squad: *"They're tombs! Also, here's a 3D model of Khufu's dental records."*

Spiritual Gang: *"They're cosmic antennas! Also, can I charge my aura here?"*

Pyramids: *"¯_(ツ)_/¯"*

Reconciling Empiricism with Vibes: A Love Story

Science and spirituality have been beefing longer than Drake and Kendrick. But here's the plot twist: they need each other.

- Science brings the receipts: carbon dating, muon scans, and the crushing reality that the Sphinx's nose was *not* stolen by Napoleon.

- Spirituality brings the *~mystique~*: secret chambers, alien architects, and the hope that maybe—*just maybe*—your soul is as eternal as a pyramid.

Together, they're like a buddy-cop movie: *"One's by-the-book! The other's high on ayahuasca! This summer... they're solving HISTORY."*

Speculative Futures: If the Hall of Records Was Real

Let's play *What If?* with the enthusiasm of a kid who just discovered caffeine:

*Scenario 1: *The Hall of Records is found.* Inside:*
- Atlantis's Yelp Reviews: *"1/5 stars – sank too fast, buffet was mid."*
- Thoth's Diary: *"Day 4,872: Still immortal. Still bored. Invented sudoku."*
- A Stone Tablet: *"Made you look. – Sincerely, The Ancients."*

*Scenario 2: *It's a dud.* Just dust, a dead scorpion, and a sticky note:*
- *"The real Hall of Records was the friends we lost along the way."*

Either way, Twitter explodes. Elon Musk buys Giza. The History Channel rebrands to *The Prophecy Network*.

The "Mytho-Science" Framework: Because Why Not?

Let's invent a new field where everyone's a little right and a little high:

Mytho-Science 101:

- o Quantum Spirituality: *"The chamber both exists and doesn't until you open it. Schrödinger's Void."*
- o Alien Archaeology: *"Sure, aliens built the pyramids... as a summer internship project."*
- o Conspiracy Therapy: *"We'll never know the truth, but here's a stress ball shaped like the Sphinx."*

Academics will hate it. Instagram influencers will *love* it.

The Pyramids' Greatest Lesson: Stay Curious, Stay Wild

At their core, the pyramids are a giant middle finger to oblivion. They scream: *"REMEMBER ME!"* in a universe that's 99.999% void. So whether you're:

- Scanning muons like a tech wizard,
- Chanting mantras to Thoth's LinkedIn profile,
- Just vibing because you got lost on a tour...

···you're part of the same human quest to yell *"WHAT DOES IT ALL MEAN?!"* into the void.

A Call to Action (But Chill, It's Optional)

Let's start a Pyramid Peace Summit:

- Archaeologists bring peer-reviewed papers.

- Conspiracy theorists bring "evidence" (read: YouTube links).
- Tourists bring sunscreen and questions like *"Where's the bathroom?"*

www.ingramcontent.com/pod-product-compliance
Lightning Source LLC
Chambersburg PA
CBHW070442010526
44118CB00014B/2152